Y0-BBY-137

CANCELLED
BOOK SALE

Copyright © 2016 by Kevin Mincher
All rights reserved.
Published in the United Kingdom by Unstoppable Teen Ltd.

ULTIMATE YOUTH LIFESTYLE

How any teenager can have more confidence, more happiness and more success

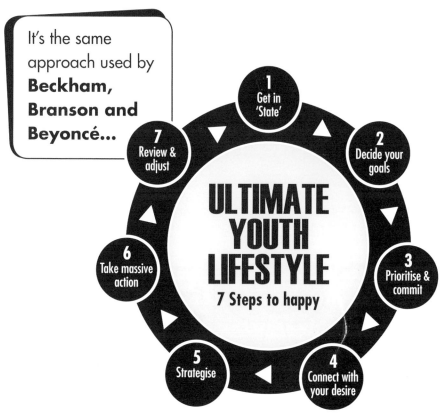

It's the same approach used by **Beckham, Branson and Beyoncé...**

ULTIMATE YOUTH LIFESTYLE
7 Steps to happy

1
Get in 'State'

2
Decide your goals

3
Prioritise & commit

4
Connect with your desire

5
Strategise

6
Take massive action

7
Review & adjust

You've finally found it...

...the mini-book that's designed for those new to Unstoppable Teen (UT for short), and for those committed UT enthusiasts who want a refresher on the fundamental principles of youth empowerment.

YOUTH EMPOWERMENT

To enable young people to deal with their problems and achieve their goals.

To move beyond their current issues and take control of their own destiny.

What follows is our road map. It's how we help teenagers overcome their challenges and experience more happiness.

You see, all young people are at various levels of needing some kind of help. There's soooooo much to learn, and so little time to do it! (We don't just mean school learning. We mean life learning too.)

From 13–19, we are attempting to improve ourselves and get better at the things that matter to us. We want to have lots of fun and enjoy our carefree freedom, but we also want to get ready for the next chapter of our lives.

Enjoy the present

Prepare for the future

We're not little kids anymore, but we're not fully independent grown-ups either. There seems to be this constant balancing act between enjoying our youth and preparing for adult life.

Many of us struggle to get that balance right. Some of us spend so much time looking for ways to make progress that we forget to enjoy what remains of our youth. Whilst others of us are so focused on having a good time that we miss valuable opportunities to get ahead.

Before we go any further...

You need to know this isn't your typical book because we aren't your typical youth organisation. We like to do things differently!

I almost didn't publish this because various people told me it was too short to be a 'proper book' and teenagers wouldn't have the interest or discipline to stick around and read it.

I disagreed.

It's my experience that young people will go the extra mile to improve their own lives when they understand the importance of something.

I've worked with more than 300,000 teenagers, so I've got lots of experience to draw upon.

I've seen students turn up for extra lessons before school, after school and during their holidays to get those extra few percentage points that will enable them to get the grades they want. I've seen them join clubs, groups and teams... all in the quest to have more fun and achieve more success.

According to a study by the U.S. Bureau of Labor Statistics, this is how teenagers spend their time...

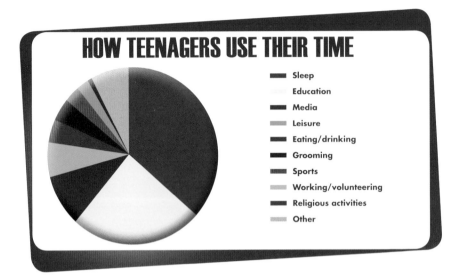

HOW TEENAGERS USE THEIR TIME

- Sleep
- Education
- Media
- Leisure
- Eating/drinking
- Grooming
- Sports
- Working/volunteering
- Religious activities
- Other

Teenagers spend an average of 6.8 hours on their own education every day. That's huge!

I'm confident that plenty of teenagers (particularly those dedicated to having the best life possible), will happily spend some of that time reading this book.

Oops!

The truth is, I started out with the intention of writing a short article about how we help teenagers. I wanted to share the steps you can take to improve your life during your teenage years.

But I got a little carried away, (that happens a lot!) and I ended up writing a mini-book!

This will take you roughly an hour to read.
Obviously that depends on how quickly you read and how long you take to think about the content as you go.

You don't have to read the whole thing in one sitting,
but you can if you want to! Many people read one section at a time, and complete the whole thing over several days.

I'll cover some of the most important foundations in the first half.
Then I'll build on that in the second half by giving you the simple steps you can take to create the life of your dreams.

(I'll be sure to put little notes throughout the article to let you know when it's a good time to take a break.)

I refuse to dumb things down

I won't treat you like a kid and patronise you just because you're a teenager. I want you to have all the details that really matter – so that's what you're going to get.

If you're like the thousands of other teenagers I've had the privilege of helping, I know how much you value:

- Your confidence
- Your education
- Your relationships
- Your health
- Your hobbies
- Your community
- Your career
- Your future
- Your life!

If you prefer to get your information in tiny bite-sized chunks, I encourage you to visit our social media channels because that's where we post short-form content every day.

 facebook.com/unstoppable.teen

 twitter.com/unstoppableteen

 instagram.com/unstoppableteen

You might also want to checkout our blog (unstoppableteen.com/blog) and podcast (unstoppableteen.com/podcast) because we share #TopTips for teenagers every week.

Are you committed to having the best life possible?

If you're still reading, you're clearly one of those people who is dedicated to having the best life possible.

Frankly, spending an hour reading an article is the minimum you can expect to invest in yourself and gain positive results in return.

If you can't be bothered to do that, you probably have unrealistic expectations about what it takes to be happy and successful.

Right, let's get started!

Adolescence is a time of dramatic change and personal transformation – like no other phase in our lives. Life was so simple during childhood. But then the teenage years arrive and bring mammoth changes…

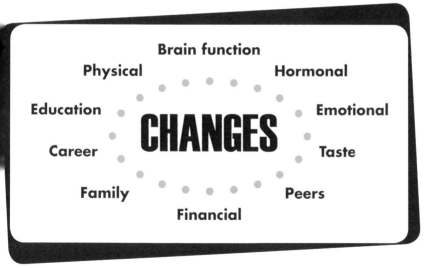

In today's world, the demands on teenagers quickly ramp up and the pressures intensify. It comes from everywhere – home, school, friends, teams, clubs, groups, employers, social media, celebrities, politicians – you name it, the expectations relentlessly rain in.

New responsibilities are identified and there's so much to adapt to within such a short period of time. It's unsurprising that with so much going on, so many young people struggle to cope.

We have shocking levels of under-achievement in high school, eating disorders, self-harming, obesity, anger issues, drug and alcohol abuse, unemployment, depression and suicide amongst young people.

It doesn't have to be this way

The transition from childhood towards adulthood can be filled with great joy and achievement. This page is here to help you optimise those teenage years – to thrive in the present and rise to new heights in the future.

The system

This is the same approach David Beckham, Sir Richard Branson, and Beyoncé used to accomplish astonishing things in their teenage years. It's how Nelson Mandela, Oprah Winfrey and Malala Yousafzai came through challenging childhoods to upgrade the world around them. It's how J.K. Rowling, Mark Zuckerberg and Will Smith became household names.

This approach works if you have a high IQ,
and it works if you score lower on that scale.

It works if you're currently doing well in school, and it works if you're not.

It works if you have lots of money, and it works if you who haven't got as much as you'd like.

It works if you have clear goals for the future, and it works if you haven't got a clue what you want to do yet.

It works if you're experiencing personal problems, and it works if your life has been plain sailing thus far.

This approach works because it uses the irrefutable laws of success put forth by legendary researchers and leaders throughout history.

As Steve Jobs once said...

You don't just live in life. You change it. You shape it. You make your mark upon it.

The question is...

How do you do that? How do you create a life you love? And how do you do it in an enjoyable way?

The answer lies in what we call the Ultimate Youth Lifestyle or UYL.

Read this page carefully. Read it multiple times and commit it to memory. I encourage you to take notes as we go because that will help you maximise the benefits for your self and the people you care about. This is the stuff they don't usually teach you in school.

Things are NOT as they seem...

There isn't one UYL.

We aren't here to tell you how to live your life. That's for you, and only YOU to decide.

The fact is there are many ways to experience a happy life.

Sadly, study after study has discovered that fewer than 20 per cent of adults are happy with their lives.

That means a WHOPPING 80 per cent of adults are NOT happy.

How can this be?

How can so many human beings be messing up their lives?

One thing's for sure…

I don't want you to repeat the mistakes of previous generations. I formed Unstoppable Teen because I want to help young people avoid the mistakes of the past and experience a great life.

When I say, "Ultimate Youth Lifestyle", some people think I'm referring to what teenagers do in their leisure time, the places they hang out, the fashion brands they wear, their hobbies, and the amount of disposable income they have.

But that's NOT what I mean.

If you look up the word *lifestyle* in the dictionary, you'll discover a definition like this…

Lifestyle

The attitudes, decisions, behaviours and habits that together form the way an individual lives.

So, when I refer to Ultimate Youth Lifestyle, I mean the attitudes, decisions, behaviours and habits that are PROVEN to help young people experience better life outcomes, such as:

- Better confidence
- Better grades
- Better relationships
- Better health
- Better careers
- Better life!

You see, it's your attitudes, decisions, behaviours and habits that ultimately create your experience of life. If you take control of these things, you will take control of your life, and the amount of success and happiness you experience.

It's worth repeating we aren't here to tell you how to live your life. We certainly aren't here to be your guru.

Simply put, we are here to be your CHEERLEADER and SHARE valuable insights that can help you experience a better life.

What you do with that information is entirely up to you.

Learn the steps of the Ultimate Youth Lifestyle

The following diagram outlines our UYL approach.

Download a PDF version at unstoppableteen.com/ultimate-you-lifestyle.

Print this PDF version and put it on your bedroom wall, next to your desk or somewhere else you will see it regularly. If you intend to improve your life by implementing this plan, you'll need to refer to it often.

When you're learning new strategies for upgrading your results, you'll need to remind yourself of the UYL process. Otherwise you'll probably waste time and make unnecessary mistakes.

This is a warning: There is little point in just intellectually understanding success strategies like goal setting, effective study skills, and visualisation techniques. There is enormous benefit when you apply these methods to the UYL process and turn them into personal habits.

Here is a flowchart of the Ultimate Youth Lifestyle process...

ULTIMATE YOUTH LIFESTYLE
7 steps to happy

1 Get in 'State'
Your emotions have a huge affect on your decisions, so get in a positive state of hope and optimism before making decisions about your life.

2 Decide your goals
It's your life and it's for you to decide how you're going to enjoy it. Don't follow the crowd. Instead, set goals based on your own strengths and passions.

3 Prioritise & commit
You can achieve anything, but you haven't got time to do everything. So make positive choices about what you most want to experience in your life.

4 Connect with your desire
Happiness isn't easy – if it was, everyone would do it. By unleashing and maintaining your motivation, you'll keep moving forward when the going gets tough.

5 Strategise
Anything is possible when you break it into small enough parts. So develop a personalised plan that enables you to take daily steps towards your goals.

6 Take massive action
Those who achieve the most, are those who do the most. You need to develop enjoyable daily routines and rituals that create the results you want.

7 Review & adjust
We rarely reach our goals with our first attempt. Those who self-reflect, learn from experts, and change their ways are most likely to succeed.

Here are the steps…

1. Get yourself into a state of hope and optimism. Whilst in that state…

2. Decide your goals – choose things you want to experience in life that excite and inspire you

3. Prioritise and commit to the things you value most

4. Connect with your desire in order to unleash your inner motivation

5. Strategise – Have an effective plan for getting what you want

6. Take massive and consistent action towards your goals

7. Regularly review your progress and make adjustments where necessary

Get stuck into this article and pay close attention because we're about to reveal the details of the exact process we use to empower young people and help them experience the life they want, including…

✓ Stronger self-esteem and belief
✓ Higher grades in school, college and university
✓ Better relationships with family and friends
✓ Enhanced physical health
✓ More fun and happiness
✓ Career success in business, entertainment and sports

…and that's just to name a few.

Before we get into the detail of the 7 steps, there are some things you need to know…

Self-led improvement

You cannot rely on schools and the government to give you EVERYTHING you need for a fantastic future. They simple cannot do it all.

You need to accept responsibility for your own life, take control of the situation, and equip yourself with the skills you need to create the life you want.

Some people think that's a bit harsh and young people should be left to just enjoy their lives. But let me ask you something…

When is the right age for people to become responsible for their own lives?

In my country, Great Britain, you can vote when you're 18… which means lawmakers believe you're responsible enough to affect the governance and direction of the nation by that age.

You can learn to drive when you're 17… which means lawmakers believe you're responsible enough to control a vehicle travelling at high speed, and be trusted to protect the lives of your passengers and other road users.

You can legally have sex when you're 16… which means lawmakers believe you're responsible enough to become a parent and raise a family, because that's the ultimate consequence of having sex!

Blame and wait for others ▶ ▶ Accountable and self-led

So…

With these things in mind, when do you think you should start learning to be responsible for your own attitudes, decisions, behaviours and habits – the very things that lead to your results and experience of life?

Perhaps it's a personal thing that needs to be determined on a case-by-case basis.

One thing's for sure…

Without being responsible and accountable for your own life, you have absolutely NO chance of consistently experiencing happiness and success.

The best you can hope for is fleeting moments of goodness because you'll be constantly looking for others to blame when things go wrong.

You certainly won't be looking for ways to improve your own circumstances until you become accountable for your own progress.

The beauty of accepting responsibility for your own self-led improvement is that you take control of your own life – you put your happiness in your own hands – and that is incredibly empowering.

(This is a good place to take a break if you want to. Otherwise, plough ahead because I'm about to share something that's pivotal to your future success and happiness.)

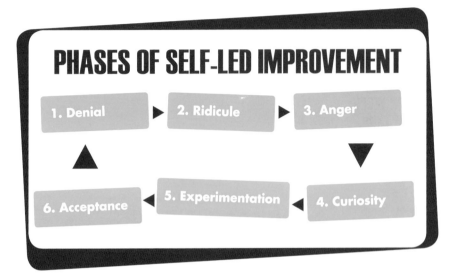

PHASES OF SELF-LED IMPROVEMENT

1. Denial ▶ 2. Ridicule ▶ 3. Anger

▲ ▼

6. Acceptance ◀ 5. Experimentation ◀ 4. Curiosity

Whilst we might be impatient and want aspects of our lives to improve instantaneously, the reality is that it takes time for us to do it.

Here's a brief explanation of the 6 phases of self-led improvement that I often share with students and teachers in my school seminars:

1. DENIAL

In phase one we've got our head buried in the sand. We are oblivious to the fact that there are things we can do to upgrade our own lives (including our school grades, stress levels, and social life, etc.). Even when there are decisions and actions that can be taken to improve the situation, people who are in denial don't think it's their responsibility to do it. They say things like...

"It's not my fault."
"There's nothing I can do."
"I've already tried everything."
"It's impossible."

2. RIDICULE

Phase two is the calm before the storm. It's when those in denial move towards ridiculing and mocking the self-improvement suggestions being made to them. They do this in the hope they won't have to accept responsibility and get on with the task of improving their own results. They say things like…

"What a stupid suggestion."
"That will never work."
"It's a waste of time."
"What's the point? It won't last."

3. ANGER

You might want to bring your boxing gloves for phase three because things can get a little heated! When those in denial realise their jibes were ignored and their ridicule didn't work, they can start to feel threatened and insecure. In their last attempt to avoid responsibility for their own improvement, their defences go up. Some people go quiet and experience an inner rage. Others go on the attack. You'll here them say things like…

"Leave me alone."
"What's it got to do with you?"
"Who do you think you are to suggest such a thing?"
"I don't need you or anyone else telling me how to live my life."

4. CURIOSITY

In phase four, the denial, ridicule and anger subsides, and people get curious about the options available to them. It's like you're sat beside an enchanting moonlight campfire. Inspirational thoughts and dialogues begin to flow. People start asking questions and exploring ways they might be able to take their own life to the next level. You'll here them say…

"What are my options?"
"How have other people done it?
"What do the researchers and experts suggest?"
"I'm not saying I'll do it, but how did you do it?"

5. EXPERIMENTATION

In phase five, we arrive at the exciting part. It's as if a tempting ocean of opportunities stretches out ahead of us, and people dip their toe in the water to discover which life-improving ideas work for them. Their curiosity tips into action, which gives them a chance of experiencing better results. People in this phase say things like...

"Let's give it a go."
"I'm not saying I'll do it forever, but I'll try."
"Do you fancy doing it with me?"
"This might actually work."

6. ACCEPTANCE

Finally, in phase six, we take control of the things we used to be in denial about. Our experiments turn into enjoyable activities that produce positive results. We now have new ways of doing things that bring us great joy and success. These habits become embedded in our life and form the 'normal' way we do things each day. It starts to feel like home. People in phase six say things like...

"That's just the way we do things around here."
"It's one of my habits. It's part of my routine. It's who I am."
"Isn't this the way we've always done it?"
"I can't remember it ever being any different!"

Interestingly, just when you think you've got everything figured out, something else shows up to make you realise you've still got room for growth, and the six phases of self-led improvement start again... just in a different area of your life!

Where are you on this journey towards self-led improvement and creating your Ultimate Youth Lifestyle?

If you've moved beyond denial, ridicule and anger… and you're moving towards the part where you're curious about what you can do to take your life to the next level… and you're willing to experiment with new ways of doing things… you're ready for the 7 steps of the Ultimate Youth Lifestyle.

(I suspect you're ready because you probably wouldn't have visited our website if you weren't… and you certainly wouldn't have read this far into this article!)

These are the exact steps I used to make my own dreams come true.

(Including: achieving double the national average grades in school, playing professional football, traveling around the world, and starting my own award-winning business… all before my 21st birthday).

These are also the exact steps I've used time and time again to help thousands of students experience their Ultimate Youth Lifestyle.

So let's crack on…

STEP 1: GET YOURSELF INTO A STATE OF HOPE AND OPTIMISM

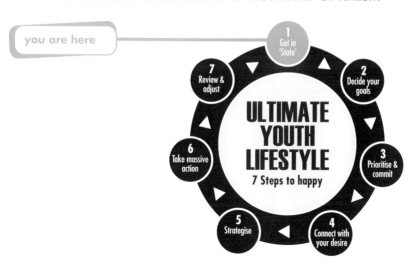

Lots of teenagers make the mistake of rushing ahead to step 2 before they've taken care of step 1. That's a HUGE ERROR.

Your first priority is to get yourself in a POSITIVE emotional state BEFORE you do anything else because your emotions have a significant impact on your decisions and actions… which in turn lead to your results.

"An optimist is someone who expects his dreams to come true; a pessimist expects his nightmares to." Laurence J. Peter – educator

When we feel fearful, stressed and insecure, we make completely different decisions compared to when we feel hopeful, optimistic and confident.

When in a negative state, it's proven that parts of the brain perform worse, which means we use less of our intelligence and skills.

This is why you should never make important decisions about your life or set goals when you're in a state of fear or negativity (e.g. anxious about upcoming exams, concerned about not being good enough to get in to your first choice college, or worried about what your family and friends might think about the career choices you're making).

In those emotional states it's inevitable you'll make choices that are far less than you're capable of.

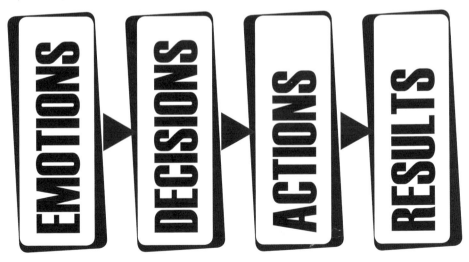

Just to emphasise this point…

It is ESSENTIAL that you lead yourself into a POSITIVE emotional state BEFORE you go to step 2.

BELIEVE IN YOURSELF

Make sure you're feeling hopeful and optimistic before you make any decisions and choose what you want in your UYL. This will help you choose authentic targets that genuinely motivate and inspire you.

Studies by Gallup discovered that students who have hope for the future tend to achieve more than their classmates who don't have hope for the future.

Gallup defines 'hope' as, 'The ideas and energy we have for the future.'"
After conducting research with thousands of students they found…

THE IMPORTANCE OF HOPE

✔ **Hope drives school attendance**
✔ **Hope predicts high school grades**
✔ **Hope predicts retention in post-16 education**
✔ **Hope scores are most robust predictors of higher education success than high school grades**

The evidence is overwhelming. Those of us who have hope for the future are likely to achieve more than those who don't.

There's a plethora of simple strategies you can use to get yourself into this powerful emotional state. One of the easiest and most enjoyable methods (that teenagers love) is to listen to your favourite uplifting music.

For more easy-to-implement ideas, check out the techniques in our TURBO, BOOST and BELIEVE programmes. You can access these coaching videos in our membership area (unstoppableteen.com/membership/).

Once you've got yourself into a positive state of hope and optimism, you're ready to move on to the next part of the Ultimate Youth Lifestyle process. So let's build some momentum and move on to...

STEP 2: DECIDE YOUR GOALS

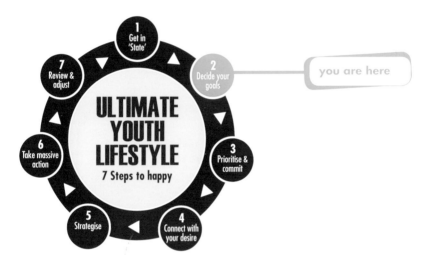

Life is pretty simple...

Human beings want to spend more of their time experiencing positive emotions (like happiness, love, confidence and success), and less of their time experiencing negative emotions (such as boredom, loneliness, anger and depression).

Thankfully, we are born with an incredible power to MAKE DECISIONS and shape our own lives. Sadly, many teenagers surrender this power.

This step of the Ultimate Youth Lifestyle is all about you reclaiming that incredible power. It's time for you to start making positive decisions about what you want to have, do and be in your life.

"People with clear written goals, accomplish far more in a shorter period of time than people without them could ever imagine." Brian Tracy – entrepreneur and best-selling author

Super successful people set goals... create targets for themselves... have aims and objectives... aspirations for the future... a mission... call it whatever you want!

Quite simply, you need to have something positive to look forward to in your life. And you're the person who needs to decide what that's going to be. After all, it's your life! So it needs to be YOU who decides what you're going to do with it (not your parents, the government or anyone else).

WHAT WOULD YOU DO IF IT WERE IMPOSSIBLE TO FAIL?

Many teenagers don't have goals that inspire them. Others do have goals, but don't truly believe they can reach them.

It's time to move beyond those limitations and other issues that prevent teenagers from achieving their potential.

I believe we ALL deserve to live a happy life. I also believe Albert Einstein was right when he said...

"Everyone is a genius. But if you judge a fish by its ability to climb a tree, it will live its whole life believing it is stupid."

Many teenagers fall into the trap of conforming to social stereotypes and others' expectations (e.g. boys have to be good at sports and girls are supposed to be good at dancing).

We have to move beyond these outdated restrictions and expand our perceptions of what's possible.

You might not be surprised to know that when young people are asked to reveal their top goal for the future, the most common answers include:

- I want to be rich
- I want to be famous

The same teenagers are rarely able to identify what they're going to do in order to become rich and famous. And when quizzed further there's a lack of depth in their thinking about what they intend to do with their wealth and fame once it's been earned.

Other common mistakes include:

1. Misunderstandings about what it really takes to enjoy and win the game of life, which leads many teenagers to set inappropriate goals such as, 'Get drunk with my friends'.

2. Setting goals that aren't related to the individual's strengths and passions, which make them almost impossible to attain.

3. Lack of creativity shown through an inability to choose different targets to their family, friends and the norms of their community (e.g. 'My dad was an accountant so I'm going to be an accountant').

4. Giving up their power to make decisions by putting things off, passing the buck and refusing to set goals. Sometimes teenagers do this as an act of rebellion, but they only cause themselves harm.

5. Decisions being made by parents, friends, teachers and others, rather than teenagers themselves. This often leads to a life of boredom, frustration and regret.

6. Not having an effective strategy for deciding what you want to experience in your UYL and making it happen. They might have 'wishes' and 'dreams' but no clear road map for making them real.

7. Unwilling to go outside one's comfort zone and try new things, which prevents teenagers from having new experiences and improving their lives.

8. Being pessimistic and constantly focusing on how things could go wrong (e.g. 'I have no talents and there's nothing fun to do around here').

9. Negative people, media and personal surroundings that brainwash teenagers into believing they can't succeed.

10. Lacking the health and energy required to turn their dreams into reality.

11. Fear (including fears of failure and, on the other hand, worries about what the downside might be if they actually succeed).

12. Learned helplessness: believing that no matter what they do, it won't make a difference to their situation.

Which of these mistakes have you experienced in the past? And what other errors can you add to the list?

Almost everyone struggles with one or more of the above issues at some time during adolescence. The good news is you can move beyond these challenges, become self-led, and create a better lifestyle for yourself.

12 principles of effective goal setting

It's time to leave those problems behind and move forward towards a brighter future. It's time for you to start making positive decisions about what you want in your future. It's time for you to design your Ultimate Youth Lifestyle.

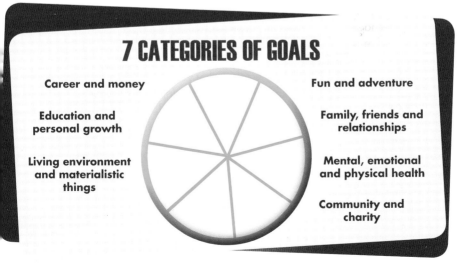

7 CATEGORIES OF GOALS

Career and money

Fun and adventure

Education and personal growth

Family, friends and relationships

Living environment and materialistic things

Mental, emotional and physical health

Community and charity

Remember, there isn't one 'Ultimate Youth Lifestyle'. Don't follow the crowd. Tread your own path and decide what you want to be, have, and experience.

- ✓ Learning to surf
- ✓ Fluent in a foreign language
- ✓ Mastering a musical instrument
- ✓ Joining a sports team
- ✓ Graduation
- ✓ Passing your driving test
- ✓ Winning an award
- ✓ Round the world trip
- ✓ Raising money for your favourite charity
- ✓ Getting your dream job

It's all out there waiting for you.

#Toptip: If you ever get stuck for ideas, you might find it useful to go online and search for 'bucket list ideas'. You'll find countless links to inspirational sites and pages that will show you all kinds of amazing things other young people around the world have done.

You might also want to check out our series of blog articles called, 101 Top Teen Bucket List Ideas (unstoppableteen.com/101-bucket-list-ideas-teenagers/). You're bound to find some inspirational stuff you probably never thought of, but that you'd love to do.

Here are a dozen more #TopTips to help you design your UYL:

1. Keep in the forefront of your mind that you deserve the BEST in life.

2. Know that irrespective of your past, you can have a fantastic future.

3. It's your life, so it's up to YOU to decide what you're going to do with it.

4. Choose goals that excite you, inspire you, and that you will ENJOY pursuing.

5. Make decisions that enable you to play to your personal STRENGTHS and PASSIONS.

6. Select some materialistic 'things' you'd like to own, but also decide on some brilliant life experiences you'd like to have.

7. You don't need to know HOW to achieve a goal at the time you set it. You just need to know you WANT it.

8. Have small goals that might be easy to reach, and have big goals that will require you to push further than ever before.

9. Have short-term goals that you can attain within a month or two, and have long-term goals that might take you years or decades to accomplish.

10. Be specific. Saying you want 'good grades' isn't sufficient. What specific grade do you want in which specific subjects?

11. Don't focus exclusively on one area of your life (e.g. your school grades). That's boring! It's important to have exciting goals for different areas of your life.

12. At least a tiny part of you needs to BELIEVE it's possible to reach the goals you choose.

There are dozens of ways to decide what you want in your Ultimate Youth Lifestyle. Some people like writing lists, whilst others like putting pictures on their walls of the things they want. What's important is that you find a process that works for you.

We've created a FREE guide called, *38 Ways Celebrities Set Goals And Succeed… And How You Can Do It Too!*, to help you learn about the different methods you can use to design a delicious future for yourself. Check it out and discover which approach is best for you…

38 WAYS CELEBRITIES SET GOALS & SUCCEED

(... AND HOW YOU CAN DO IT TO

UNSTOPPABLE TEEN
HELPING YOUNG PEOPLE EXPERIENCE BRILLIANT LIVES

DOWNLOAD NOW

(This is a good place to pause if you want to. To maximise your benefits, I encourage you to complete the steps above before you read further.)

After you've identified all the things you want to accomplish as part of Ultimate Youth Lifestyle, you're ready for…

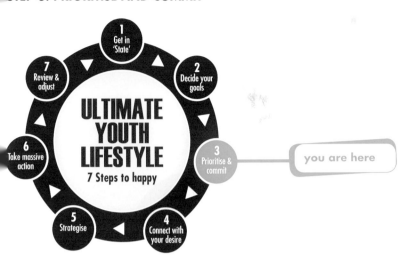

After completing step 2 correctly, you'll have lots of fab things you want to have, do and become in your future.

It's exciting!

Indeed, for some teenagers, it can become too exciting and they become overwhelmed by the sheer number of amazing things they want to experience.

When that happens, many people procrastinate. They have this incredible list of things they desire, but they never get started.

I don't want that to happen to you.

As Oprah Winfrey famously said…

"You can have it all. Just not all at once."

Oprah Winfrey – billionaire media mogul

When we're young we're often impatient to get the things we want. We want it all and we want it now! But that's not how the Ultimate Youth Lifestyle works. We need to learn the importance of patience and prioritisation.

Day in and day out I meet teenagers who overestimate what they can do in 6-12 months, but underestimate what they can accomplish in a decade.

These teenagers naively think they can graduate high school, pass their driving test, start their own business, earn their first million, visit every continent on the planet, run a marathon, raise $100,000 for charity, fall in love, and become a pro athlete... this year!

Okay – maybe I'm exaggerating! But you get my point, don't you?

Average life expectancy in Britain and many developed countries is now above 80 years. Some experts are predicting that one in three of today's teens will live beyond their 100th birthday. Which means we have plenty of time to do great things with our lives.

Now that you've set some goals for your UYL, you need to consider how you're going to phase those experiences.

7 questions to help you prioritise and commit

1. Which of your goals play to your personal strengths and passions?

2. Which of the experiences would bring you the most happiness?

3. Which of your intentions excite you the most?

4. Which of your objectives will you be most proud of when
    you achieve them?

5. Which of your aims do you need to pursue first because they
    will enable you to pursue the next ones on your list?

6. Which of your targets would you willingly get up before
    6am in order to pursue?

7. Which parts of your UYL would you pursue, knowing that
    even if you failed, you'd have a great time?

It's essential that you take time to consider which of your aspirations are your top priorities for the next 12 months, and which ones can be put on hold for a while.

I recommend you have a maximum of four top targets you're going to focus on for your Ultimate Youth Lifestyle this year. Ideally, you'll select different categories of goals for different areas of your life.

There's nothing worse than focusing entirely on your education and career, at the total expense of your relationships and hobbies. That's like going out for a mouthwatering meal and only having a starter and main course, but never having drinks or dessert (which are often the best bits!).

So choose targets that will give you balance and all-round happiness as you pursue them.

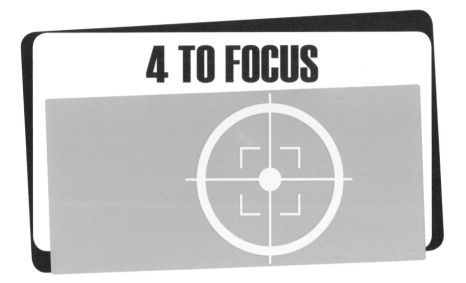

4 TO FOCUS

The success principle we're applying here is that in life...

WE TEND TO GET WHAT WE FOCUS ON.

The human brain isn't designed to focus on dozens of different things at the same time. Teenagers become more productive and more successful when we focus our time, energy and resources on a few things that we really want.

So make some choices, then, make a COMMITMENT to yourself to accomplish those aims. That's what self-led teenagers do.

Prioritise the elements of your Ultimate Youth Lifestyle that inspire you and give YOU hope for your future. Focus on the things that make you want to work hard every day because you want them so much.

I'm fed up of hearing teenagers talking about flaky dreams and their wishy-washy preferences for the future. In a whiny and weak tone of voice they say things like...

"I hope I get good grades."
"It would be nice if I had more confidence."
"It would be lovely if I got my dream job in the future."

NO!

These are pathetic statements that lack the certainty and COMMITMENT required to achieve your Ultimate Youth Lifestyle.

STOP IT. NOW. .

Don't tease yourself with false hopes.

Let's take a look at that word…

COMMITMENT
To express one's intention.
To pledge oneself to a position.
To engage. To perform. To do.
To make a promise.

You need to shut off from all other possibilities and resolve yourself to reaching your UYL. Don't give yourself any get-out clauses.

Look at how we've re-worded the previous whiny sentences with more certainty and conviction…

"I WILL get good grades."
"I am building my confidence."
"I'm on a mission to get my dream job."

Say these phrases to yourself with the tone of dedication and determination in your voice. Feel the power it gives you when you fully commit to something.

Decide, right now, that you are absolutely going to do whatever it takes to reach your goals. Then you're ready for…

STEP 4: CONNECT WITH YOUR DESIR

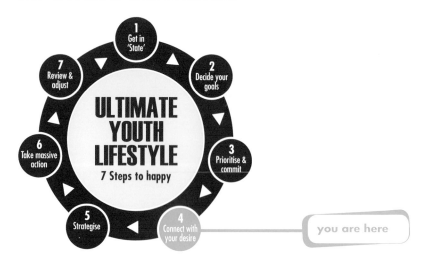

If you understand and do this step, you'll be ahead of most teenagers.

GRIT and DETERMINATION trumps IQ and natural smarts. In other words, those of us who keep going when the going gets tough, will tend to achieve more than others who are cleverer but quit during times of adversity.

People talk about the importance of resilience, but you've got to have something worth being resilient for. That's why we did such a thorough job of choosing goals that inspire you in steps one to three above.

"The will to win, the desire to succeed, the urge to reach your full potential... these are the keys that will unlock the door to personal excellence."
Confucius – philosopher

Lots of teenagers waste their time hoping bad things won't happen when they're pursuing their UYL. Let me explain why this is such a catastrophic error.

- There will be times when things are going well and you're surging ahead
- There will be times when you feel stuck and making no progress
- There will be times when you regress and fall backwards

That's life!

The fact is EVERYONE experiences difficulties and makes mistakes whilst pursuing their UYL. You will get tired, you will feel confused, you will be frustrated, you will get criticised, you will experience rejection, you will hit the wall…

It's all part of your journey to success.

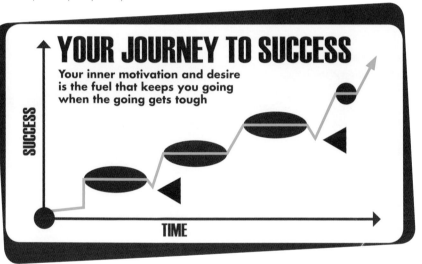

Those of us who know WHY we want to achieve our goals and are connected to our inner MOTIVATION will keep going when the going gets tough.

Those of us who aren't connected to our inner motives are likely to quit…
and there's only one thing that happens to quitters.

The tiniest amount of talent backed up with tons of tenacity is enough to help you experience your Ultimate Youth Lifestyle. You have to WANT it. Really WANT it in your heart and soul. So…

Be clear about WHY you want your UYL

Not why your parents want it. Not why your teachers, friends or the government want it. But why do YOU want it?

Answering to the following questions will help you unleash your motivation and be resilient when times get tough.

1.   What will it ultimately cost you if you don't achieve your aims?

2.   What do you ultimately stand to gain by reaching your biggest dreams?

It's worth considering:

- What will happen to your self-belief?
- How will your family and friends respond?
- What will your teachers and coaches say?
- What will happen to your health?
- What will happen to your level of wealth?
- How will it affect the things you own?
- Where will it take you?
- How will it affect where you live?
- What impact will it have on your time?
- How will it influence your personal growth?
- How will it shape your daily lifestyle?
- What will happen to your happiness?
- How will it make you feel?

Keep your answers to these questions in the forefront of your mind as you pursue your Ultimate Youth Lifestyle because they will give you the energy required to realise your ambitions.

If you discover that you don't really want the goals you chose, you need to go back to step 1 and start the process again. Next time, be sure to choose goals YOU really want.

Remember, the going will get tough. But don't get dispirited when your chips are down because it's all part of the process. Lead yourself through those challenges.

Desire is the fuel that will enable you to find answers when your journey seems impossible. It will provide the power that will propel you towards your UYL.

So stay connected to your inner hunger and thirst for success. Feel it every day. Let it flow through your veins, then move on to…

STEP 5: STRATEGISE

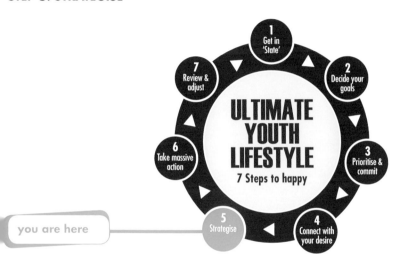

At this point you're probably raring to go. But I want to help you avoid a common mistake that causes many teenagers to fail.

We all know the importance of hard work. However, if you work hard at the wrong things you'll never experience your Ultimate Youth Lifestyle.

Imagine climbing to the summit of a mountain, only to discover your ropes were attached to the wrong mountain!

That's why it's essential to take some time to determine an effective strategy that will lead you towards your top targets. You need to create a plan that, when implemented, will lead you from where you are to where you want to be.

"Failing to plan is planning to fail."
Alan Lakein – author

Having a well-thought plan enables you to save time and work smarter. It's the road map that guides you in the right direction and ensures you're working hard at the right things. It will keep your daily efforts focused on the things that will take you step-by-step to the success you want.

The question is, how do you create a plan to achieve something you've never achieved before?

The answer is simple…

GET EXPERT ADVICE

The quickest route to your Ultimate Youth Lifestyle is to get expert advice and implement their PROVEN methods.

An 'expert' is someone who has already achieved what you want to achieve. If you want to achieve a grade 'A' in mathematics, find someone else who's achieved that grade and ask them how they did it.

You don't need to reinvent the wheel. Somebody already knows how to produce the results you want. You need to find these people and learn from their valuable experiences.

"When you have a mentor who puts no limits on your potential, the future starts to look a lot bigger and more exciting."
Melinda Gates – business woman and philanthropist

This #TopTip will help you avoid embarrassing mistakes, enable you to save huge amounts of time, and get you to your UYL much quicker than if you try to figure it all out on your own.

Of course, not everyone you ask for help will be gracious and give you the answers you're looking for. But rejection is a normal part of your journey to success. Get over it, move on, and ask another expert for their help instead.

The quality of the questions you ask during this step will determine the quality of your strategy. Here are some basic questions you need to ask an expert so you can speed up your success:

1. What did you do?
2. Who did you do it with?
3. Where did you do it?
4. When did you do it?
5. How did you do it?
6. Why did you do it?

Here are 18 advanced questions that I like to ask when I meet experts (the answers I get help me eliminate errors and accomplish more than others think is possible):

1. What emotional states are you in when you're pursing the goal?
2. Which emotional states do you avoid?
3. What do you observe, listen to and pay attention to that helps you succeed?
4. What do you ignore?
5. What thoughts do you think?
6. What questions do you ask yourself?
7. What are your attitudes and beliefs?

8.   What are your values? What is most important for you to avoid? What is most important for you to gain and experience?
9.   What do you do with your body and physiology?
10. Who do you work with? Who is on your team? How do you work together?
11. Who do you communicate with? How do you communicate?
12. What equipment and resources do you use?
13. What strategies, techniques and methods do you use?
14. What are your daily routines and rituals? How do you sequence your actions?
15. What do you not do, that causes other people to fail?
16. What do you do that is different from a person who is not successful?
17. What is the difference that makes the difference?
18. What drives you?

The answers you get to all of the above questions need to form the basis of your plan for how you're going to create your Ultimate Youth Lifestyle. They will help you break your big goals down into smaller manageable parts. And that's great news because anything becomes possible when you chunk it into small enough tasks.

#TopTip: Just in case you can't find an expert or mentor to help you, know that you can always find answers to the above questions by reading books (especially autobiographies and self-help books), watching videos (especially documentaries), listening to podcasts and audio books, and completing research online.

The answers are out there. You just have to lead yourself to them.

(This is a good place for you to pause if you want to. Feel free to take as much time as you need to complete the previous steps. I don't want you to just understand this stuff. I want you to actually experience your Ultimate Youth Lifestyle… and that requires you to implement the things you're learning here.)

Once you're organised with your personal action plan, you're ready for…

STEP 6: TAKE MASSIVE ACTION

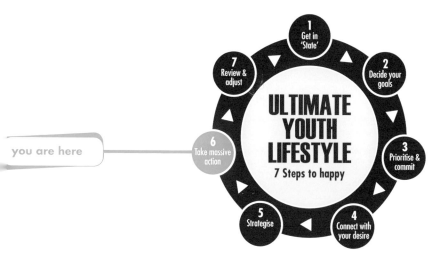

you are here

The strategy you outlined in step 5 will only be as effective as the quality with which you implement it.

Too many teenagers fall into the trap of putting off until tomorrow, that which they could have done today. These folks shouldn't be surprised when they don't reach their Ultimate Youth Lifestyle.

"You must take action now that will move you towards your goals. Develop a sense of urgency in your life."
H. Jackson Brown Jr. – best-selling author

Each day we have an opportunity to do remarkable things and make our dreams come true.

Youth empowerment is simply about leading yourself from your current reality (where you are now) to your desired reality (the goals you set for yourself in step 2).

When you are aware that you can improve your life and you want to do it, the question then becomes, are you willing to do whatever is necessary to make it happen? And are you willing to do it NOW?

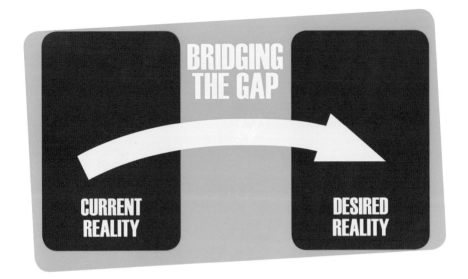

It saddens me that some teenagers just aren't prepared to work hard enough, for long enough. They want it all, and they want it now. But that's not how it works.

The UYL is a marathon, not a sprint. There are NO quick fixes.

Great effort leads to great rewards. I think most people intuitively know this to be true. They might not want it to be true, but in their heart of hearts, they know it's true.

How can you possibly expect the best grades, the best friendships, the best fun and the best lifestyle if you don't give the best of yourself each day?

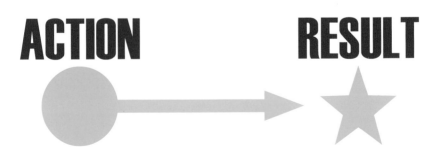

Every result you ever experience is preceded by your actions.

Your current scores in school, your level of confidence, the quality of your relationships, the amount of money you have in your bank account, your level of health… all of these things were determined by YOUR actions in the past.

The results you experience in the future will be created by the action you're taking today. So, now you've got a vision for your UYL and you've got a plan, it's time to put your energy into implementing that plan.

FOCUS ON WHAT YOU HAVE TO DO TO SUCCEED, RATHER THAN THE RESULT ITSELF.

After working with more than 300,000 teenagers, I've come to realise there are four types of teenager:

i.   Those who don't have any goals.

ii.   Those who have hopes but don't do anything to make them happen.

iii. Those who have targets and start taking action, but don't sustain their efforts over time.

iv.   Those who have aspirations, start taking action, and sustain their efforts until they reach their aspirations.

Which one are you?

The greatest rewards are experienced by those teenagers who put forth the greatest EFFORT.

It's about work ethic, hustle and stamina. These are the muscles you must develop over time because these are the muscles that will enable you to experience your greatest dreams.

Day after day, week after week, month after month, year after year… the teenagers that DO the most ACHIEVE the most.

Don't go whining to anyone that, "It's hard." Of course it's hard!

"If it wasn't hard, everyone would do it. It's the hard that makes it great."

Tom Hanks – award-winning actor

Have the courage to go outside your comfort zone and do those things that might seem difficult at first. When you do this regularly, your self-belief and inner strength will soar to new heights.

The daily discipline of focusing your energy and efforts on the relentless pursuit of your UYL is of utmost importance. Make the accomplishment of your goals your priority every day.

The key to sustaining your efforts over time lies in your ability to find ways to ENJOY what you're doing.

3 #TOPTIPS TO HELP YOU ENJOY TAKING ACTION

1. Know that there's a way to make anything fun. It all depends on how creative you're prepared to be. For example: you can be boring and do all your studying at a desk, or you can be creative and do some studying in a tree or hot tub instead!

2. Open your mind and don't follow the crowd. Ask yourself, 'How can I do this and enjoy the process?'

3. It feels less like work and more like fun when you're pursuing goals you truly care about. So if you're not enjoying your efforts, perhaps you should think about choosing some different goals.

You'll spend thousands of hours working hard and pursuing your goals. So you may as well figure out a way to enjoy the journey. Indeed, that journey is your life. So don't wish it away.

The moment of victory is so short and often passes in a moment or matter of minutes. If that's all you're living for, you're kind of missing the point. The Ultimate Youth lifestyle is all about enjoying each day. Carpe diem. Seize the day!

STRONGER TOGETHER

Take your friends and family on the journey with you. It's always more fun when you've got someone to share the experience with. It's also easier to overcome difficulties when you've got someone to spur you on. You know the saying, 'A problem shared is a problem halved'.

You might be like me and have to go it alone for a while because your current mates aren't quite so self-led and immediately up for the challenge.

That's ok because you'll make new friends along your path to success. In time, your current friends are likely to follow your lead because they'll want to taste some of the success you'll be experiencing.

After you've gotten yourself into the pattern of taking massive action on a daily basis, it's important that you regularly…

STEP 7: REVIEW AND ADJUST

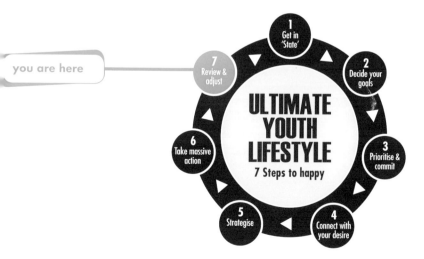

In this step you accept responsibility for the consequences of your actions, take time to learn lessons that will help you, then move forward with your mission.

If you're getting the results you want, you need to CELEBRATE, reward yourself, and keep doing what you're doing.

But what will you do if you're not getting the results you want?

DID YOU KNOW...

- 10 publishers rejected J.K. Rowling's first Harry Potter book before Bloomsbury decided to print it. Harry Potter went on to become one of the best-selling book and movie series of all time. It turned J.K. Rowling into one of the wealthiest women in the world.

- More than 100 banks refused to lend Walt Disney the money he needed to build Disneyland. Thankfully he persisted and eventually opened what became the most visited theme park on the planet, attracting more than 650,000,000 visitors!

- Edison made 1,000 unsuccessful attempts at inventing the electric light bulb before he got it right. Imagine a world without electric light... Many people would have quit way before he figured out that life-changing invention.

Each of these people understood that failure is part of success.

I want more teenagers to wake up to this fact and change their attitude towards failure because we rarely hit the jackpot first time. In all probability, it's going to take many attempts before you experience your Ultimate Youth Lifestyle.

Saying you want success without failure is like saying you want pancakes without eggs! You can't have pancakes without eggs. And you can't have success without failure.

The fact is you're human, and all humans make mistakes. None of us is perfect. GET OVER IT!

Errors and embarrassments are inevitable. So don't fear or avoid them. Accept them as part of your journey to success. Work through them (in all their forms), and this will lead you to the results you desire.

It isn't the end of the world if you make a fool of yourself on a date, flunk a test or fall short in an interview. You're still alive and you have the power to make self-led improvements that will enable you to grasp the next opportunity that comes your way.

Delays are not denials, and failure isn't permanent unless you allow it to be. Slow progress and negative results provide valuable lessons that can help us succeed, if you're open to the hidden messages.

It doesn't take an award-winning scientist to figure out that if you're not experiencing your Ultimate Youth Lifestyle, you need to change what you're doing. Or maybe it does…!

"Insanity is doing the same thing over and over again expecting different results."
Albert Einstein – award-winning scientist

Frustratingly, many teenagers are set in their ways. They want their parents to change, they want their teachers to change, they want their friends to change, they want the government to change… but they don't want to change themselves!

As they old saying goes…

If you always do what you've always done, you'll always get what you've always got.

One thing I've noticed over the years is that teenagers who are flexible with their thoughts and behaviours tend to be more successful than those who are set in their ways.

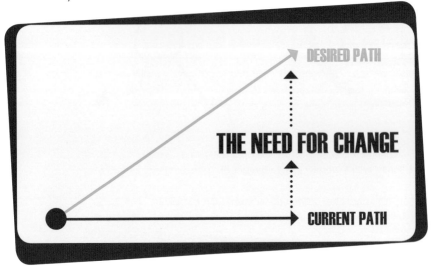

If you're flexible, you'll find ways around any problem that shows up. If you stay stuck in your ways, it's unlikely you'll discover the solutions that will lead you to glory.

That begs the question…

How many times will you change your approach in order to achieve your goals and live your ultimate lifestyle?

I hope your answer was, 'As many times as it takes!'

Two ways to figure out what you need to change and improve

Here are a couple of suggestions that will help you speed up your progress:

1) SELF-REFLECT

Having accurate self-awareness is essential for anyone who wants to experience their Ultimate Youth lifestyle. You've got to know what you're good at, and it's essential you know what you need to improve.

The truth will set you free. So be honest with yourself.

Don't beat yourself up (e.g. 'Everyone hates me and nobody will ever be my date for the prom'). But don't big yourself up either (e.g. It won't help to kid yourself you're in line for a grade 'B' if all the tracking data shows you're currently heading for a 'D').

Those who delude themselves deny themselves opportunities improve and succeed. Those who are honest with themselves open the door to possibility and progress.

I recommend you think about the action you've taken (and not taken). Think about what worked (and didn't work). It's important to consider:

Immerse yourself in the details of your journey so far and take time to consider how you can take your self-led improvement to the next level.

Potential questions you might think about include:

- Did you choose appropriate goals for yourself?
- Are you playing to your strengths and passions?
- Did you do everything on your action plan?
- What actions, techniques and strategies have helped you make the most progress so far?
- What challenges have you already overcome?
- What are the most important lessons you've learned so far that will help you and others succeed in the future?
- What actions have you been putting off?
- What have you been unwilling to do or try that might improve your results?
- What and/or who distracted you?
- Did you maintain a positive mental attitude throughout?
- Did you have unrealistic expectations about how easy/hard it was going to be?
- How effective were you at controlling your emotional state?
- How well did you deal with setbacks, rejection and failure?
- What was missing from your action plan?
- What are the main obstacles you still need to overcome?
- What do you need to remove or eliminate from your life so it doesn't hold you back?
- What inner conflicts or confusions do you need to resolve?
- Have you maintained high energy levels or did you get tired?
- Are you giving your body the rest, nutrients, hydration and exercise it needs every day?
- What equipmeni or resources are you lacking?
- Which negative attitudes and beliefs do you need to let go of?
- What positive attitudes and beliefs do you need to strengthen?
- What do you need to start that you weren't doing before?
- What do you need to do more of that you were doing before?
- What do you need to do less of that you were doing before?
- What do you need to stop doing completely?
- What do you need to learn?
- Which skills do you need to upgrade?
- What advice do you need to get? What do you need help with?
- Who could help you? Who do you need to add to your team?
- Who do you need to remove from your team?
- What have you enjoyed so far?
- What could you do to enjoy it even more?

There's a lot to consider, but the more detail you go into, the easier it will be to make faster progress and reach your Ultimate Youth Lifestyle.

That's why it's super helpful to…

2) GET FEEDBACK FROM EXPERTS

You already know the fastest route to success it to copy the mindset and methods used by experts who have already achieved the results you want.

The assumption I'm making is that you're COACHABLE and OPEN to receiving that advice. I shouldn't make that assumption because many of us foolishly think we know everything, even though we don't.

This ignorance and arrogance has catastrophic consequences because it prevents you learning what you need to move forward.

"I was 16 years old. I thought I knew everything, but I knew nothing."
Rita Ora – singer

Thankfully, we can all wake up to the fact that we've got room to grow and improve. When you have that epiphany you'll discover the knowledge and support you need is all around you. It might be in unexpected places, but it's there waiting for you.

When you're ready to make progress and experience your UYL, I encourage you to start asking questions. Reach out to teachers and experts – ask them for their feedback and insights.

#TopTip: I answer teenagers' questions in my Unstoppable Teen weekly podcast. It's FREE coaching without the cost of one-to-one help. So send me your questions via Facebook, Twitter or Instagram and I'll be happy to help wherever I can.

Feel free to use the questions I outlined earlier as a useful start point, and design your own questions to get the information you need – whether that's from me, or others who can help you.

Just remember that the quality of your questions will determine the quality of your answers. So take your time with this step and gather the distinctions that will enable you to create your UYL.

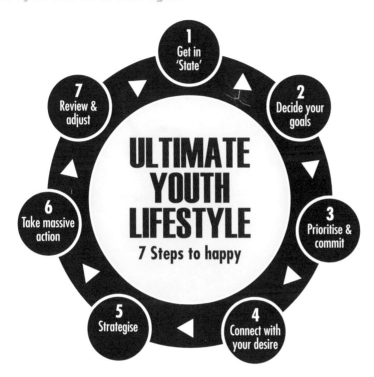

The Ultimate Youth Lifestyle is really a never-ending journey of self-led improvement. Once you've completed the seven steps, you start the cycle all over again! It's a continuum that I repeat three times every year.

Depending on the size of the goals I'm pursuing, it typically takes me a weekend or up to a week to complete steps one to five.

I then immerse myself in the process of taking massive action every day (step 6) for 3–4 months.

Finally, I use a week at the end of that period to reflect on my progress (step 7), before making necessary adjustments and starting the cycle over again.

My year looks something like this…

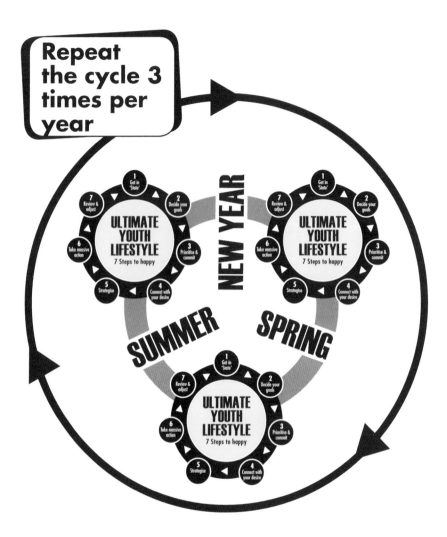

Some people say I was lucky to achieve double the national average grades in school, play professional football, travel to 40+ countries around the world, build an award-winning business, and have such a loving family and group of friends.

But they're wrong. The truth is I wasn't lucky at all. I've been using these seven steps to create my own ultimate lifestyle since I was a teenager. The system works!

You can do it too

Congratulations on reading this mini-book from cover to cover! Whether you did it in one sitting, or took breaks along the way, you invested in your own self-development… and that deserves great praise.

I believe with all my heart and soul that life doesn't happen to us, it happens for us. Every teenager can experience his or her Ultimate Youth Lifestyle.

The single most impactful action you can take right now is to set yourself up with a person or organisation that will give you regular guidance to help you create the life you want.

If you want to learn more about how we help young people here at UT, and get more in-depth coaching about the Ultimate Youth Lifestyle that we've covered here, you can download the FREE Unstoppable Teen App via Google and Apple.

This FREE App is packed with content to help you improve five important areas of your life:

1) Emotional fitness and psychological strength
Including how to build your self-confidence, reduce stress and be more resilient.

2) Physical health and wellbeing
Including how to boost your body image and energy levels.

3) Learning and thinking skills
Including how to improve your memory and achieve higher grades in school.

4) Communication and leadership
Including how to talk to anyone and become an influential person in your community.

5) Financial intelligence and career success

Including the habits of millionaires and insights from top achievers around the world.

All of this and a whole lot more!

We share new content with teenagers, their friends and families every week... and it's **ABSOLUTELY FREE!**

If you've read this far, I know you'll love our resources and you'll be stunned by the benefits you receive.

Take action now... and become unstoppable!

Thanks for reading and being part of our unstoppable community.

Notes:

Notes:

It works!

"Your advice was brilliant and it helped me to get into college."

Nathan, 17

"Kevin has helped me by showing me how to take responsibility for my actions and enjoy problem solving."

Dylan, 18

"I liked the advice and it gave me lots of confidence to keep working hard."

Azumi, 14

"I thought I had to follow a boring career path that I did not particularly want to do just because people have labeled me as "clever". I have been dancing all my life and now am going to become a professional dancer! You have changed my life, thank you so much!"

Shay, 16

"It really helped me see how to reach my goals and dreams."

Megan, 18

"You've drastically changed my life. I wouldn't be doing what I am without you putting into perspective what I could be. Thank you!"

Brad, 15

"Kevin opened my eyes to a lot of things and made me realise what I can do in my school years to achieve my potential."
Jack, 15

"That man knocked some sense into me."
Luke, 15

"I just want to say thanks because I've started looking into my interests to see what sort of careers I can get out of them. I have begun to write my own novel and I have told my parents that one day I will buy a pig!"
Magic, 17

"You gave me a perspective on what I want to do and how to reach my goals, thank you!"
Alex, 17

"It has made me think that I really want to do something and keep on trying so thank you for helping me see straight and to know that I can do it."
Jade, 16

"I just wanted to say a big thank you because you've open my eyes and my mind and I feel so inspired and it's all because of you. I truly believe I can do anything I put my mind to and I'll face the obstacles head on. Thank you so much for motivating me and making me believe in myself."
Maddison, 16

Now it's your turn!

Get FREE inspirational help every week!

The Unstoppable Teen Blog

Celebrity success stories | Teen achievements | Latest research and advice
Read and subscribe at www.unstoppableteen.com/blog

The Unstoppable Teen Podcast

Weekly ideas and insights to help young people
experience more success and happiness.
Listen now at www.unstoppableteen.com/podcast

Subscribe on: